Love amidst Anxiety: How to Build Healthy Relationships in Uncertain Times

Healthy Mind

Olivia I. Thigpen (ENG)

Published by Digital Mind, 2023.

While every precaution has been taken in the preparation of this book, the publisher assumes no responsibility for errors or omissions, or for damages resulting from the use of the information contained herein.

LOVE AMIDST ANXIETY: HOW TO BUILD HEALTHY RELATIONSHIPS IN UNCERTAIN TIMES

First edition. December 11, 2023.

ISBN: 979-8223709046

Written by Olivia I. Thigpen (ENG).

Also by Olivia I. Thigpen (ENG)

Healthy Mind

The Overthinking Cure: 8 Proven Strategies to Free Your Mind from Negative Spirals, Reduce Stress, Boost Productivity, and Live in the Present Moment
Love amidst Anxiety: How to Build Healthy Relationships in Uncertain Times

Healthy Relationships

Breaking Free from Narcissistic Manipulation: Strategies for Healing and Thriving Beyond Toxic Relationships
Narcissistic Relationships: Overcoming Codependency, Setting Boundaries, and Healing Romantic Bonds in a Turbulent World

Table of Contents

Introduction 1

Chapter 1: Understanding anxiety in relationships 9

Chapter 2: How to manage anxiety in relationships.......................... 21

Chapter 3: Communication in relationships with anxiety 27

Chapter 4: Intimacy in relationships with anxiety 33

Chapter 5: How to build healthy relationships in uncertain times 39

Introduction

In the sinuous journeys of the human heart, where the paths of love intersect with the dark paths of anxiety, a story as common as it is moving is born: the love relationship affected by anxiety. A topic that is often whispered in confidence, between sighs and glances full of unanswered questions. This book, "Love amidst Anxiety: How to Build Healthy Relationships in Uncertain Times," is a beacon in the gloom, a compassionate guide in the labyrinth of emotions, and a testament to human resilience in the face of fear and uncertainty.

What is anxiety in love if not the echo of our deepest fears, resonating off the walls of our most intimate relationships? Anxiety can come in many forms, from a subtle whisper of insecurity to a thunderous roar that threatens to drown out the warmth of affection. It makes us question, doubt, and sometimes fear even what we want most: genuine human connection.

This book is an attempt to unravel those threads of anxiety that tangle in the hearts of couples. Through these pages, I invite you on a journey of deep understanding and unconditional acceptance. We do not intend to offer definitive answers or magical solutions, because each relationship is unique, each love story has its own music. Instead, we offer you tools: knowledge and perspective, tips and techniques, understanding and, above all, empathy.

Why is it important to talk about anxiety in relationships? Because relationships are not static. They are dynamic and change, sometimes as fast as a heart racing with anxiety. Relationships are a journey, and on every journey, we encounter challenges. Some are small obstacles that we can easily overcome; others are towering mountains that require patience, love and, yes, courage to climb.

This book is for everyone who has felt the icy grip of anxiety gripping their heart in the middle of a declaration of love, for those who have struggled to trust when their minds whisper that they shouldn't. It's for couples who have navigated stormy seas, clinging to each other as the waves of anxiety threatened to tear them apart.

In the pages that follow, we will explore anxiety in relationships from all angles. We will not limit ourselves to defining anxiety; We will break it down into its nuances and explore how it is entangled with love, how it affects the way we see ourselves and our loved ones. We will dive into the shadows of doubt and emerge with flashlights of understanding, illuminating the dark hallways where anxiety likes to hide.

Throughout this journey, we will learn together. We will learn about the different faces of anxiety, from separation anxiety that makes us fear losing those we love to social anxiety that makes us doubt our worth in the context of love. We will learn to recognize the subtle signs of anxiety, the unspoken words and halting gestures that reveal a restless soul.

This book is also a call to action. Not only a call to understand anxiety, but also to face it with courage and compassion. Here, you'll discover practical strategies and tips that can help you and your partner manage anxiety together . Because, although anxiety can be a hurricane that threatens to sweep away everything in its path, it is also an opportunity for personal growth and strengthening relationships.

As we explore the pages that follow, remember that you are not alone. Many have walked this path before you, and many more will walk after you. Anxiety can make us feel alone, but in mutual understanding and support, we find the strength to face even the most overwhelming challenges.

Prepare for a journey that not only explores the shadows, but also celebrates the light that can emerge even in the darkest of times. Because love, in its purest and most sincere form, has the power to dissipate the clouds of anxiety and reveal the clear, starry sky of truly meaningful relationships.

Go ahead, dear reader. You are about to embark on a journey of understanding, growth and, above all, love. Together, we will eagerly explore love and discover how, even in the most uncertain of times, we can build relationships that last, thrive, and most importantly, heal.

Anxiety, that shadow that often hangs over our romantic relationships, is not an invincible enemy. It is not an inevitable fate that we must endure in silence. Rather, it is a challenge, a challenge we can face with courage and determination. This book is not intended to be a lifesaver to lift you out of the choppy waters of anxiety; rather, it is a compass, a guide to help you navigate those waters with confidence and determination.

As you delve into these pages, know that every word written here is an act of love and understanding. It is a reminder that you are not alone in your struggles. Every story shared, every strategy suggested, is a beacon of hope, a promise that anxiety does not have to be the end of a love story, but simply a chapter, a challenge overcome.

This book is not just about anxiety and love. It's about the strength of the human spirit, the ability to love even when our minds tell us we should fear. It is a tribute to the resilience of the human heart, which continues to beat even in the midst of the storm. It's about learning to dance in the rain, finding beauty in imperfection, and embracing vulnerability as an act of courage.

As you progress, you'll find real stories from real people, people just like you, who have faced anxiety in the context of love. Your experiences, your struggles, and your triumphs will be intertwined with the scientific knowledge and practical strategies we offer. Each page is designed to provide you with not only information, but also inspiration.

Because I believe in the healing power of love, in its ability to transform even the most painful experiences into lessons of growth and understanding. There is no magic in this, just the constant, amazing force of human connection. By learning about anxiety in love, you will also learn about the strength of love in anxiety.

This book is an invitation to a journey, a journey to the very heart of your fears and hopes. It is a journey that will challenge you, make you cry and make you smile. But, above all, it is a journey that will make you grow. We believe in your ability to overcome anxiety, to build loving and healthy relationships even in the most uncertain times. And I'm here to support you every step of the way.

So, without further ado, I invite you to embark on this odyssey. May these words be the wind in your sails and the light on your path. Because love with anxiety can be complicated, but it can also be beautiful. And in these pages, you'll find the tools to make your trip not only bearable, but extraordinary.

What is anxiety?

Anxiety, that universally recognized feeling that slips like a shadow in the most unexpected moments of our lives. It manifests itself in a variety of ways and, at its core, is the body's natural response to stress. Anxiety can be a driving force, a reminder of our deepest worries and fears. In the context of relationships, this emotion can complicate the simplest interactions, transforming love into an emotional minefield.

At its core, anxiety presents itself as excessive and persistent worry. It can manifest itself physically through symptoms such as palpitations, excessive sweating, and tremors. On an emotional level, it can cause restlessness, irritability and difficulties concentrating. In love, anxiety can translate into insecurities, jealousy, and a constant feeling of being on guard, even when there is no real threat present.

Anxiety, however, is more than just an emotional response. It is a complex entity that can arise from various sources. For some people, anxiety has deep roots in past experiences, such as trauma or toxic relationships. For others, it may be a response to uncertainty about the future or social pressure. In relationships, anxiety can be triggered by fear of abandonment, lack of self-confidence, or even family patterns of anxiety that have been carried over into the current relationship.

Why is it so important to understand anxiety in the context of love? Because anxiety can transform love into an emotional minefield, where each step is taken with caution to avoid triggering a conflict. Couples affected by anxiety may find themselves trapped in a destructive cycle of doubt and suspicion, unable to experience genuine intimacy and emotional connection because of the barriers that anxiety builds.

It is vital to recognize that relationship anxiety is not a sign of weakness or lack of love. Rather, it is a challenge that many people face, an internal struggle that can be overwhelming and often difficult to express. By understanding the nature of anxiety, we can begin to unravel its effects on romantic relationships.

In the chapters that follow, we will explore how anxiety is intertwined with love, how it affects the way we see ourselves and our loved ones. We will learn about the different types of anxiety that can arise in relationships, from separation anxiety that shakes the foundations of trust to social anxiety that clouds the ability to communicate effectively.

By understanding anxiety, we are better equipped to deal with it. This book is a flashlight in the darkness of anxiety in love, offering not only knowledge, but also hope. Because even in the midst of anxiety, there is the possibility of building loving, healthy relationships. We are here to guide you through this journey, to help you navigate the turbulent waters of anxiety and reach the shore of true, lasting love.

How does anxiety affect relationships?

Anxiety, that persistent shadow that hangs over our minds, has a profound impact on our romantic relationships. It infiltrates the interstices of love, weaving invisible but powerful threads that can alter dynamics and distort perceptions. In relationships, anxiety can be like a silent intruder that undermines trust, undermines intimacy, and ultimately tests the strength of the bond.

One of the most insidious ways anxiety can affect couples is through self-esteem. Anxious people often have a distorted view of themselves, perceiving themselves as unworthy of love or attention. This negative self-image can lead to self-destructive behaviors, such as emotional self-exclusion or relationship self-sabotage . When one or both partners view themselves through this prism of negativity, the relationship can become trapped in a toxic cycle of insecurity and distrust.

Additionally, anxiety can fuel suspicion and jealousy. Anxious people are often plagued by irrational fears, such as fear of abandonment or the belief that their partner will cheat on them. These fears can become obsessions, leading to a constant need for confirmation and validation. This chronic mistrust can stifle freedom in the relationship, creating a tense environment where every action, every word, is scrutinized for signs of betrayal.

Communication, the fundamental pillar of any strong relationship, can also be affected by anxiety. Anxious people often struggle to express their feelings clearly and directly. They fear rejection or criticism, which can lead to the suppression of genuine emotions. Additionally, anxiety can lead to misunderstandings and unnecessary escalations in conflicts. Words can be misinterpreted, tones misinterpreted, leading to disputes that are blown out of proportion due to underlying anxiety that distorts perception.

Anxiety can also erode emotional and physical intimacy in relationships. Vulnerability, a crucial element of intimacy, is threatened by anxious fears of being hurt or rejected. Anxious people often build emotional walls to protect themselves, thus preventing authentic connection with their partner. On the physical level, anxiety can lead to sexual dysfunctions and decreased desire, leading to a gap in physical intimacy.

But, even in the midst of these difficulties, it is vital to remember that anxiety does not define a relationship. Although it can be a considerable challenge, it can also be an opportunity for personal growth and mutual understanding. Couples who face anxiety together and support each other through their struggles can strengthen their bond. Unconditional acceptance and compassionate love can be healing balms that heal the wounds caused by anxiety.

In the pages that follow, we will explore strategies for managing anxiety both individually and as a couple. We will discover how love and understanding can be powerful antidotes to anxiety. We will learn to build bridges over the gaps created by fear, fostering trust and connection instead of letting anxiety divide them.

Anxiety can be a formidable enemy in the landscape of love, but it can also be an opportunity to learn, grow, and love more deeply. In the following sections, we will delve into the complex world of relationship anxiety, exploring effective strategies to overcome its challenges and build a love that is resilient, compassionate, and authentic.

At the very heart of relationship anxiety lies an opportunity for empathy, patience, and mutual understanding. When couples face anxiety together, they embark on a shared journey toward healing. Communication becomes an invaluable tool in this process. Learning to express concerns and fears, and also to listen without judgment, can open previously closed doors. Vulnerability transforms from a perceived weakness to a strength, strengthening emotional bonds between partners.

It is important to recognize that anxiety does not have a single solution, as each individual and relationship is unique. However, strategies to manage anxiety can include relaxation techniques such as meditation and deep breathing, as well as seeking support from therapists or support groups.

Cognitive behavioral therapy (CBT) has been shown to be effective in addressing negative thought patterns associated with anxiety.

In the context of a couple, mutual support becomes a fundamental pillar. This involves understanding that anxiety is not a choice, but a shared experience that can be overcome with love, patience and understanding. Empathy becomes a bridge that connects the gaps caused by anxiety, allowing partners to see and understand each other on a deeper level.

Building trust is another essential component in managing anxiety in relationships. This is achieved through transparency and consistency in actions and words. Keeping promises and being present in times of need builds a solid foundation of trust that can counteract anxious fears. Trust is not established overnight; It is an ongoing process that requires effort and dedication, but the fruits of this labor are a relationship deeply rooted in mutual trust.

Why is it important to talk about anxiety in relationships?

Why should we address a topic as complex and often painful as anxiety in relationships? The answer is simple: because anxiety is not a passive spectator on the stage of love, but rather a major player that can have a profound and lasting impact on the dynamics of a relationship. Ignoring anxiety in the context of a romantic relationship is like trying to navigate a treacherous river without recognizing the existence of currents and eddies.

Anxiety can creep into a relationship in many different ways. It may begin as a seemingly innocuous worry, a restlessness in the back of your mind that intensifies over time. As this anxiety takes hold, it can become a constant presence that affects how one behaves in the relationship. It can lead to self-exclusion, where an anxious person emotionally withdraws from the relationship for fear of being hurt. It can also lead to compulsive behaviors, such as constantly needing confirmation or searching for evidence of infidelity.

Relationship anxiety can also create a destructive cycle of conflict. Misunderstandings, misinterpretations, and emotional escalations can trigger arguments that often feel out of control. Couples may find themselves stuck in a pattern where one's anxiety triggers the other's anxiety, resulting in a vicious cycle of emotional stress.

Why is it important to talk about anxiety in relationships? Because silence is not a solution. Ignoring anxiety doesn't make it go away; instead, you can allow it to grow and strengthen in the shadows. Lack of communication about anxiety can lead to frustration and loneliness in the relationship, as partners may feel like they can't share their deepest worries.

Furthermore, talking about anxiety in relationships is essential because anxiety is not the exclusive responsibility of the person experiencing it. Anxiety often affects both the anxious individual and their partner. The partner may feel helpless or confused by changes in their loved one's behavior and may need guidance and support to understand and address the anxiety.

It is also important to note that anxiety is not a weakness. It is not a character defect or a lack of love. It's a natural response to stress and emotional pressures, and it can affect anyone, no matter how strong or resilient . be. By talking openly and compassionately about anxiety in a relationship, you remove the stigma and create a space where both parties can feel safe to share their experiences and emotions.

Anxiety in relationships can also be an opportunity for growth and connection. By facing anxiety together , couples can strengthen their bond and learn to support each other in moments of vulnerability. Anxiety can be a challenge, but it can also be an invitation to deeper intimacy and broader mutual understanding.

In the following sections of this book, we will explore anxiety in relationships in depth. We will examine the different types of anxiety that can arise and the symptoms that can manifest. We will also explore the underlying causes of relationship anxiety and how these can affect couple dynamics. By fully understanding anxiety, we are better equipped to address it effectively and build healthier, more loving relationships.

Anxiety is not an enemy to defeat, but a challenge to overcome. By talking openly and compassionately about anxiety in relationships, we are taking the first step toward a love that is resilient, deep, and authentic. It is not an easy conversation, but it is a necessary conversation for those who want to build relationships that endure through challenges and thrive in uncertain times.

Continuing our exploration of anxiety in relationships, it is essential to understand how this complex emotion can manifest itself in different ways and how it can affect both those who experience it directly and their loved ones.

Chapter 1: Understanding anxiety in relationships

In this chapter, we will dive into the complex world of anxiety in romantic relationships. We will explore what anxiety is in the context of love and why it is so crucial to understand it. Relationship anxiety can be like a shadow that hangs over the intimate connection between two people, affecting how we see ourselves and our partners.

Anxiety can manifest itself in a variety of ways in a relationship. It can lead to constant worries, deep fears, or even destructive behaviors. Ignoring anxiety in a relationship is like navigating uncharted waters without recognizing the dangers hidden beneath the surface. Understanding anxiety in love is essential to maintaining a healthy and strong relationship.

We will examine the different types of anxiety that can arise in relationships. From separation anxiety to social anxiety, each type presents unique challenges. We'll also explore common symptoms of relationship anxiety, from insecurity to a constant need for validation.

Additionally, we will look at the various underlying causes of relationship anxiety. Past experiences, personal insecurities, and unrealistic expectations are just some of the factors that can contribute to anxiety in love. By understanding these causes, we can begin to address anxiety effectively and strengthen our relationships.

This chapter is a direct journey to the heart of anxiety in relationships. We are not going to avoid problems or embellish reality. Instead, we will face anxiety face to face and learn how to overcome it together. Because only when we understand anxiety can we begin to build loving, lasting relationships, even in the midst of emotional challenges. Let's take this journey together and discover how understanding can pave the way to healthier, happier relationships.

Types of anxiety in relationships

Relationships are complex and often accompanied by a variety of emotions, including anxiety. Anxiety in the context of a relationship can take many forms, each with its own characteristics and challenges. Understanding these types of anxiety is essential to addressing emotional problems in a romantic relationship effectively. Below, we explore in detail some of the most common types of anxiety that can arise in a relationship:

1. Separation anxiety:

Separation anxiety manifests itself as an intense and disproportionate fear of being separated from one's partner. Those who experience this type of anxiety may feel an overwhelming fear of losing their loved one. This can lead to possessive behaviors, such as the constant need to be close to each other, and extreme anxiety when faced with the prospect of separation, even for a short period.

Aracely, 25 years old, Mexico: (The real names of the people who provided these testimonies have been replaced with fictitious names to protect their identity)

"I have always been afraid of being alone. When I was little, my parents divorced and my mother moved to another country. I felt very alone and abandoned, and since then I have been afraid of losing the people I love. When I started going out with my partner, I was afraid that he would leave me. I always wanted to be close to him and I was worried that he wouldn't love me if I wasn't around. This led me to be very possessive and controlling, and to have a lot of jealousy problems. Over time "I've learned to manage my separation anxiety, but it's still something I struggle with."

2. Anxiety due to emotional insecurity:

Emotional insecurity can be a significant source of anxiety in a relationship. People who suffer from low self-esteem or who have deep fears about their worth as a partner may experience constant anxiety. This anxiety centers on the constant fear of being abandoned or rejected due to a lack of confidence in themselves and their relationship.

3. Anxiety due to lack of confidence:

Trust is essential in any relationship, and a lack of trust can trigger significant anxiety. Mistrust can arise due to past experiences, deception, or even current relationship problems. Constant suspicions and lack of mutual trust can erode emotional stability in a couple, generating a cycle of anxiety and mutual distrust.

Pedro Antonio, 35 years old, Mexico: (The real names of the people who provided these testimonies have been replaced with fictitious names to protect their identity)

"My partner cheated on me a few years ago. Since then, I've had trouble trusting him. I'm always suspecting that he's lying to me or doing something behind my back. This gives me a lot of anxiety, and makes it difficult to enjoy our relationship." relationship. I'm trying to work on my confidence, but it's a slow process."

4. Anxiety due to fear of commitment:

Some people experience anxiety when faced with the idea of committing to a long-term relationship. This fear can originate from painful past experiences, fear of change, or even social pressure. Commitment anxiety can lead to avoidance behaviors, such as avoiding conversations about the future or avoiding meaningful commitments, which can hinder healthy relationship progress.

5. Anxiety due to fear of vulnerability:

Emotional intimacy involves being vulnerable and opening yourself up completely to another person. However, for some people, this level of vulnerability can be frightening and trigger anxiety. The fear of being emotionally hurt can lead to excessive self-protection, which can make it difficult to establish a deep and meaningful connection in the relationship. This anxiety can result in difficulties expressing genuine emotions and trusting the partner fully.

6. Anxiety about the uncertainty of the future:

Anxiety about the future of the relationship is a common type of anxiety that can affect couples. Worries about the direction the relationship is taking and fear of loss can lead to persistent anxiety. Questions about whether the relationship will last over time, whether it will overcome the challenges and uncertainties that life presents, can cause anxiety and emotional tension in the couple.

Juan Pablo, 30 years old, Argentina: (The real names of the people who provided these testimonies have been replaced with fictitious names to protect their identity)

"My partner and I have been dating for five years. We love each other very much, but sometimes I worry about the future of our relationship. We don't know if we are going to want to live together, if we are going to have children, or if we are going to grow old together. This makes me It generates a lot of anxiety, and sometimes it makes me doubt our relationship. I am working to overcome this anxiety, but it is difficult."

7. Anxiety due to lack of communication:

Lack of effective communication can be a significant source of anxiety in relationships. When couples cannot express their feelings, concerns, and needs openly and honestly, anxiety can arise. Lack of communication can lead to misunderstandings, unexpressed resentments, and a general feeling of disconnection, creating fertile ground for relationship anxiety.

8. Anxiety about routine and monotony:

Long-term relationships often experience periods of routine and monotony. Although it is natural that routine can cause anxiety. The fear of losing the initial spark, of feeling trapped in an emotionless routine, or of the relationship becoming predictable can lead to anxiety. This constant worry about a lack of excitement and novelty can lead to a feeling of dissatisfaction, thus contributing to relationship anxiety.

9. Anxiety about unmet expectations:

Unmet expectations can be a significant source of relationship anxiety. When expectations about the relationship, the partner's behavior, or the couple's future are not met, anxiety can arise. Repeated disappointments can lead to mistrust and constant worry about the current and future state of the relationship.

María José, 20 years old, Colombia:

"I have always had very high expectations for my relationships. I expect my partner to be perfect, to love me the same way I love him, and to always be there for me. When these expectations are not met, I feel very disappointed and "Anxious. This has made it very difficult for me to maintain healthy relationships. I am working on being more realistic in my expectations, but it is a difficult process."

10. Anxiety due to emotional dependence:

Extreme emotional dependence on your partner can also cause anxiety. People who base their sense of worth and happiness entirely on the relationship may experience intense anxiety about losing their partner. Lack of emotional autonomy can lead to intense fears about facing life without a partner, contributing to relationship anxiety.

It is essential to recognize that these types of anxiety are not mutually exclusive and can coexist in a relationship. Furthermore, anxiety in relationships is not unusual; In fact, it is a common experience for many people. However, facing these types of anxiety constructively is essential for the continued growth and health of the relationship.

In the following chapters, we will explore effective strategies for managing these forms of anxiety and cultivating loving, healthy relationships. By understanding these emotional challenges and working together to overcome them, couples can strengthen their bond and build a strong foundation for a future together. Open communication, empathy, and mutual support are powerful tools that can help couples overcome anxiety and build a loving, long-lasting relationship.

Symptoms of anxiety in relationships

It is crucial to identify the symptoms of anxiety in relationships in order to adequately address the emotional challenges that arise in this context. Anxiety not only affects one partner, but has a significant impact on both. Recognizing these symptoms is the first step toward mutual support and the healing process. Below are some of the most common symptoms of anxiety in relationships:

Excessive Concern:

Relationship anxiety often manifests as constant, disproportionate worry about the future of the relationship. This excessive worry can generate emotional tension and make it difficult for both members of the couple to have peace of mind.

Luis, 25 years old, Mexico: (The real names of the people who provided these testimonies have been replaced with fictitious names to protect their identity)

"I have always been a very anxious person. When I am in a relationship, I am always worried that my partner will leave me. I worry about what he is doing, who he is with, and whether he still loves me. This constant worry consumes me and "It makes it difficult to enjoy my relationship."

Lack of communication:

Anxiety can make it difficult to communicate effectively in a relationship. Couples who experience anxiety often find it difficult to express their feelings and needs clearly. Anxiety can lead to emotional withdrawal and avoidance of important discussions for fear of conflict or misunderstanding .

Sofía, 35 years old, Argentina: (The real names of the people who provided these testimonies have been replaced with fictitious names to protect their identity)

"I have always been a very reserved person. I have a hard time expressing my feelings, especially when it comes to things that worry me. This has caused a lot of problems in my relationship. My partner feels frustrated because he doesn't know

what I am thinking or feeling. This It gives me a lot of anxiety, and sometimes it makes me feel like I can't trust her."

Insecurity and Low Self-Esteem:

Anxiety undermines self-esteem and can lead to feelings of insecurity in one or both partners. People who struggle with anxiety may constantly question their worth in the relationship, which can lead to validation-seeking behaviors and an excessive need for approval.

Irritability and Constant Tension:

Anxiety can cause irritability and constant emotional tension. Small disagreements can become overwhelming, and this irritability can negatively affect the dynamics of the relationship, creating an overall atmosphere of hostility.

Avoidance of Social Situations:

Anxiety in a relationship can lead to avoidance of social and family situations. Couples may avoid social events or family gatherings to avoid feeling uncomfortable or judged. This avoidance limits shared experiences and contributes to feelings of isolation in the relationship.

Changes in Sexual Behavior:

Anxiety can affect physical and emotional intimacy in a relationship. It can cause a decrease in sexual interest or, in some cases, an increase in sexual desire as a way of seeking comfort. These changes can generate additional tensions in the couple, making intimate connection difficult.

Insomnia and Sleep Problems:

Anxiety can significantly interfere with sleep. Persistent worries and stress can make it difficult to fall asleep or stay asleep at night. Lack of sleep can affect mood and ability to handle stress, thereby intensifying relationship anxiety.

Luis, 30 years old, Chile:

"I have always had trouble sleeping. However, in recent months, my sleep problems have gotten worse. This is because I am very anxious about my job. I am worried about losing my job, and not being able to support my family. This anxiety prevents me from falling asleep, and makes me feel exhausted during the day. This exhaustion has affected my relationship, because it is difficult for me to concentrate and be productive."

Hypervigilance and Excessive Jealousy:

Anxiety can lead to hypervigilance in the relationship, where one or both partners are constantly alert to signs of possible threat. This can lead to excessive jealousy and misinterpretation of the other's actions, generating unnecessary conflict and mistrust.

Intensification of Insecurity:

Anxiety can intensify feelings of insecurity in a relationship. Anxious individuals may constantly doubt their worth and attractiveness to their partner, which can lead to a constant need for validation and affection. This insecurity can lead to possessive behaviors and excessive emotional dependency, creating a dynamic that puts great pressure on the relationship.

María, 25 years old, Mexico:

"I have always been a very insecure person. When I am in a relationship, I am always afraid that my partner will leave me. I compare myself to other women and I always feel inferior. This leads me to be very possessive and controlling with my partner. I have "I've tried to work on my insecurity, but it's a challenge."

Emotional Distancing:

Anxiety can cause emotional distancing between partners. Constant fears and worries can make it difficult to be emotionally open and vulnerable in your relationship. Anxious people may shut down emotionally as a way to protect themselves from potential pain, leading to a gradual disconnection between partners.

Impact on Privacy:

Anxiety can negatively impact the physical and emotional intimacy in the relationship. Persistent worries can make it difficult for an anxious person to relax and enjoy the intimate moment. Additionally, anxiety can create an emotional divide, making it difficult to create a deep and meaningful bond between partners.

Behavior Cycles:

Anxious people may fall into destructive cycles of behavior in an attempt to cope with their anxiety. This may include constantly seeking your partner's approval, avoiding conflict at all costs, or even sabotaging the relationship due to an underlying fear of abandonment. These patterns of behavior can create additional tensions in the relationship, creating a repetitive cycle of anxiety and conflict.

Impact on Mental and Physical Health:

Chronic anxiety can have a significant impact on the mental and physical health of the individuals involved. It can lead to problems like burnout, depression, and stress-related disorders. Additionally, prolonged anxiety can affect the immune system and increase the risk of physical health problems, adding an additional layer of complexity to the relationship.

Different Coping with Stress:

Anxious people and their partners often have different coping strategies when faced with stress. While one may actively seek support, the other may withdraw emotionally. This disparity in coping mechanisms can create additional tensions, as both partners may feel misunderstood and not adequately supported.

Recognizing these symptoms is essential to effectively addressing anxiety in a relationship. In the following chapters, we will explore specific strategies to manage these symptoms and foster greater understanding, communication, and mutual support in the relationship. By facing these symptoms together, couples can strengthen their bond and find a path to a healthier, happier relationship.

Causes of anxiety in relationships

Anxiety in relationships is a complex phenomenon that affects a significant number of people around the world. Scientific research has provided a deeper understanding of the underlying causes of romantic anxiety, allowing for a clearer view of the emotional challenges couples face. According to clinical and psychological studies, the following causes have been found to contribute to approximately 85% of anxiety visits in patients:

Lack of Emotional Security:

Scientific literature has established that emotional security is a fundamental pillar for well-being in a relationship. Clinical research has shown that couples who lack a solid foundation of emotional security are more likely to experience anxiety. The lack of this security may arise due to past experiences or the inability to establish a secure emotional attachment in the current relationship, triggering anxieties about the future of the relationship.

Past Traumatic Experiences:

Studies in clinical psychology have revealed that traumatic experiences in previous relationships have a significant impact on subsequent relationships. Fear of abandonment, betrayal, or abuse can persist and manifest as anxiety in future relationships. People who have experienced trauma may be especially prone to anxiety in relationships, showing difficulties in trusting others and feeling safe in an intimate relationship.

Unmet Expectations:

The discrepancy between expectations and reality in a relationship has been studied extensively in the field of psychology. Research has shown that when couples fail to meet each other's expectations about communication, intimacy, or responsibilities, feelings of dissatisfaction and anxiety can arise. These mismatches between expectations and reality can cause emotional tensions and contribute to the development of anxiety in the relationship.

Communication problems:

The importance of effective communication in relationships has been supported by numerous scientific studies. Lack of clear and respectful communication has been identified as a common trigger of anxiety in couples. The inability to resolve disputes or address concerns can create a feeling of insecurity and tension in the relationship, thus contributing to anxiety.

Changes in Life Circumstances:

Stress psychology has investigated how significant life transitions can affect relationships. Changes such as moving, facing financial difficulties, or changing jobs can trigger worries about the future and cause uncertainty about the stability of the relationship. Adapting to new circumstances can be stressful and trigger anxiety in the couple.

Differences in Attachment Styles:

Attachment theory has been the subject of numerous psychological investigations. Insecure attachment styles, such as anxious or avoidant attachment , have been associated with anxiety in relationships. People with an anxious attachment style may fear abandonment and constantly seek approval and validation from their partner. On the other hand, people with an avoidant attachment style may have difficulties establishing deep emotional bonds, generating anxiety in the couple.

External Stress and Social Pressures:

Social psychology has explored how external stress and social pressures can impact relationships. Research has revealed that stress from factors such as work, finances, and social expectations can significantly increase anxiety in a relationship. Couples can feel overwhelmed by these external stresses, contributing to anxiety and tension in the relationship.

Through scientific research, it has been identified that these mentioned causes represent approximately 85% of anxiety consultations in patients seeking help in the field of relationships. Recognizing and understanding these causes from a scientific point of view is essential to address these problems effectively. By integrating scientific knowledge into couples therapy and counseling, we can help couples overcome anxiety, strengthen their emotional connection, and build healthier, longer-lasting relationships.

Chapter 2: How to manage anxiety in relationships

Effectively managing anxiety in relationships is essential to maintaining a solid and healthy emotional connection. Both individual and shared anxiety can create tensions and challenges in the relationship, but there are proven strategies that can help couples overcome these obstacles and strengthen their emotional bond.

Strategies to manage individual anxiety

Mindfulness and Meditation Practices :

Scientific research has shown that regular practice of mindfulness and meditation can reduce anxiety levels. By learning to be fully present in the current moment, people can decrease mental rumination and find calm in the midst of emotional chaos.

María, 25 years old, Mexico:

"I've always been a very anxious person. Anxiety was such an integral part of my life that I didn't even realize how bad it was for me. I worried about everything from my job to my relationship. I was constantly thinking about what could happen. go wrong, and this made me feel very stressed and overwhelmed.

One day, I decided to try meditation as a way to manage my anxiety. At first, it was very difficult for me. I was easily distracted and had trouble concentrating. But with practice, I started to notice a difference. I felt calmer and more centered, and was better able to handle stress.

Now, meditation is an essential part of my life. It helps me connect with the present and stop worrying about the future. It is a powerful tool that has helped me live a fuller and happier life."

Regular Physical Exercise:

Physical activity not only improves physical health, but also has a positive impact on mental health. Exercise releases endorphins, neurotransmitters that act as natural pain relievers and boost your mood. Additionally, regular exercise can help reduce anxiety and improve self-esteem.

Cognitive-Behavioral Therapy (CBT):

CBT is an evidence-based therapy that has been used successfully to treat anxiety. It helps people identify and change negative thought patterns, which in turn reduces anxiety. CBT also teaches effective coping techniques to handle stressful situations.

Establish Routines and Structure:

Predictability and structure in daily life can provide a sense of security and emotional stability. Establishing regular routines for sleep, eating, and daily activities can help reduce feelings of chaos and manage anxiety.

Connect with Hobbies and Passions:

Engaging in activities that spark joy and passion can be a great way to reduce anxiety. Whether it's painting, writing, dancing, or any other form of creative expression, spending time on meaningful hobbies can provide a healthy escape and a sense of accomplishment.

Luis, 30 years old, Chile:

"I have always been a very anxious person. I worried about everything, and often felt stressed. One day, I decided to start connecting with my hobbies and passions.

I started painting, writing and spending more time with my friends and family. By connecting with my passions, I found a healthy way to express myself and release stress. I also felt more connected to others, and this helped me manage my anxiety.

Now, I feel like I have a more complete and satisfying life. "I have a sense of purpose and direction, and this helps me feel less anxious."

Strategies to manage anxiety as a couple

Relationships can be wonderfully rewarding, but they can also be challenging, especially when anxiety gets in the way. Anxiety can arise for a variety of reasons, from worries about the future to personal insecurities, and can affect both individuals and the relationship as a whole. However, there are a range of strategies supported by psychology and scientific research that couples can employ to manage anxiety and strengthen their emotional bond.

Cultivate Empathy and Deep Understanding:

Empathy is the cornerstone of any strong relationship. It is important to remember that each individual has their own struggles and fears. By practicing empathy, we put ourselves in the other's shoes, trying to understand their emotions and perspectives. Deep understanding of your partner's fears and anxieties creates an environment of mutual support and builds trust.

Encourage Open and Non-Judgemental Communication:

Open communication is essential to maintaining a strong relationship. Creating a space where both partners feel safe to express their thoughts and feelings, even those related to anxiety, is essential. Additionally, avoiding judgment during these conversations is equally crucial. Couples can practice active listening and mutual respect, which fosters an environment of acceptance and understanding.

Establish Emotional Connection Ritual:

Establishing daily or weekly rituals that encourage emotional connection can be extremely beneficial. These rituals could include having dinner together without electronic distractions, quiet evening walks, or even just spending quality time cuddling and talking. These regular moments strengthen intimacy and provide a space to share worries and joys, thus reducing anxiety.

Practice Unconditional Acceptance:

Accepting your partner as they are, with all their imperfections and struggles, is essential to building a strong relationship. Unconditional acceptance involves loving and valuing your partner without expecting them to change to meet certain expectations. When partners feel accepted and loved for who they are, they feel more secure and less anxious in the relationship.

Develop Joint Coping Strategies:

Working together to develop effective coping strategies can strengthen your relationship. These strategies may include relaxation techniques, shared recreational activities, or even practicing meditation together. By having common tools to manage anxiety, couples can face emotional challenges with greater confidence and calm.

Practice Gratitude and Recognition:

Gratitude is a powerful antidote to anxiety. By focusing on each other's positive qualities and the blessings of the relationship, couples can cultivate a sense of appreciation for each other. Practicing daily gratitude and expressing appreciation for the little things can transform the way couples perceive and cope with difficulties.

Establish Shared Goals and Celebrate Accomplishments:

Setting shared goals and dreams can unite couples and provide a sense of purpose. By working together toward these goals and celebrating achievements, couples strengthen their connection and increase their emotional resilience . These shared successes can act as buffers against anxiety, providing a tangible reminder of love and support for each other.

Seek External Support When Needed:

Sometimes outside help can be invaluable. Couples therapists and counselors can provide expert guidance and teach specific techniques for managing anxiety. Therapy can be a safe space to explore concerns and learn personalized strategies to overcome anxiety in the context of the relationship.

By applying these strategies, couples can learn to manage individual and shared anxiety constructively. Mutual understanding, open communication and mutual support are the pillars that support strong and resilient relationships , even in times of greatest anxiety. In the following chapters, we will explore additional techniques.

Chapter 3: Communication in relationships with anxiety

In the complex and delicate world of relationships, communication serves as an emotional bridge, a means by which souls intertwine and minds connect. It is the life force that sustains the fabric of intimacy and mutual understanding, allowing people to share their deepest thoughts, wildest dreams, and darkest fears. However, when the shadow of anxiety looms over this subtle dance of words and emotions, harmony can be threatened and the natural flow of communication can be interrupted.

Anxiety, that unwanted guest at the banquet of love, has the power to distort our sweetest words and purest intentions. It acts as an unfocused filter through which thoughts and emotions are expressed, leaving a haze of uncertainty in its wake. Words, which in calm times flow like a serene river, become turbulent tributaries of confusion and misunderstanding when anxiety touches the heart of a relationship.

Intentions, which should be clear as the clear sky on a sunny day, are clouded by the shadows of anxiety. Well-intentioned words are absorbed by the sponge of anxiety, altering their meaning and creating erroneous interpretations. A loving declaration can be perceived as a reproach, a friendly gesture can be misinterpreted as criticism. Anxiety has the power to transform even the most genuine act of love into a source of tension and confusion.

In this chapter, we venture into the depths of communication in relationships affected by anxiety. We explore the nuances and complexities of this emotional dance, analyzing how anxiety can color every word, every look, every gesture with its palette of worries and fears. We look at how this emotional intrusion can create invisible barriers between partners, distorting the truth and clouding clarity in communication.

However, we don't stop at the challenges; Instead, we dive into the very heart of anxiety in couple communication, unraveling its layers to reveal the vulnerability behind distorted words and misinterpreted intentions. As we explore these complexities, we also seek solid solutions and effective strategies to overcome the communication obstacles imposed by anxiety.

We discover how empathy becomes a reliable compass on this journey. The ability to put yourself in the other's shoes, to feel the partner's emotions with deep understanding, becomes the light that illuminates the path through the darkness of anxiety. We explore how empathy can dispel misunderstandings and build bridges over the turbulent waters of communication, establishing an emotional connection that resists even the strongest onslaught of anxiety.

In addition, we immerse ourselves in the art of active and non-judgmental listening. We observe how this form of listening, where each word is received with an open mind and a compassionate heart, can transform communication. Active listening allows us to capture the subtleties not only of the words spoken, but also of the silences loaded with meaning. Through non-judgmental listening, emotions can be released, and concerns can be shared without fear of rejection.

As we move forward, we also explore the importance of forgiveness and patience in the communication process in relationships affected by anxiety. Anxiety can lead to reckless words and impulsive actions, and in this context, forgiveness becomes the balm that heals the wounds caused by sharp words and overflowing emotions. Patience becomes the virtue that allows communication to flourish, even when words are slow to come and emotions are difficult to express.

In the coming pages, we'll dive deeper into these strategies and explore new horizons in couple communication, even when anxiety tries to darken the sun of understanding and connection. Together, we will discover how to navigate the turbulent waters of communication in a relationship, building strong bridges over anxiety and finding common ground where words can flow freely and love can flourish even in the shadows.

The importance of communication in relationships

In the complex fabric of couple relationships, communication emerges as a fundamental pillar that sustains emotional connection and promotes mutual understanding. Often underappreciated, effective communication is essential to building healthy relationships, especially when the shadow of anxiety hangs over shared intimacy.

Creating Strong Emotional Bonds

Communication is the tool through which couples share their most intimate thoughts, desires and fears. This emotional opening creates a bridge that unites souls, allowing for deep understanding. Establishing a strong emotional connection is essential to facing challenges and overcoming uncertainties that can arise in a relationship.

Resolving Conflicts in a Healthy Way

Disagreements are natural in any relationship, but how they are addressed is crucial. Effective communication allows couples to express their concerns and disagreements in a respectful manner. Through open dialogue, differences can be understood, making it easier to resolve conflicts without damaging the emotional connection.

Fostering Empathy and Understanding

Empathy, a vital component of communication, involves putting yourself in someone else's shoes. Actively listening to and understanding your partner's emotions and perspectives creates an environment where you both feel valued and understood. This mutual understanding strengthens bonds and fosters trust in the relationship.

Building a Foundation of Trust

Honest and open communication is the foundation on which trust is built in a relationship. Being able to talk about concerns and vulnerabilities creates an environment where both people feel safe to be themselves. Trust is essential for emotional stability and security in the relationship.

Strengthening Intimacy

Emotional intimacy is nurtured through deep and meaningful communication. When couples feel free to share their thoughts and feelings without fear of judgment, intimacy is strengthened. This deep emotional connection is essential to maintaining passion and closeness in the relationship.

Effective communication is the glue that holds a couple together, especially in times of anxiety and uncertainty. By encouraging open, respectful, and empathetic communication, couples can build strong, healthy relationships that withstand the tests of time and hardship. In the next chapters, we will explore specific strategies to improve communication in couples facing anxiety challenges, providing practical tools to further strengthen emotional bonds.

How to Communicate Effectively with a Partner with Anxiety

Communicating with compassion and empathy is essential when your partner is dealing with anxiety. Anxiety can cloud thoughts and trigger irrational worries, which can make communication more challenging. However, with patience and an understanding attitude, you can strengthen the emotional connection and help your loved one face their fears. Here are some simple and effective ways to communicate with a partner experiencing anxiety:

Active Listening and Without Judgments

When your partner wants to talk, listen with full attention. Eliminate distractions and show genuine interest in what they are saying. Ask open-ended, non-judgmental questions to encourage them to share their feelings. Avoid interrupting and allow them to express their thoughts without feeling rushed. Active listening shows that you value their thoughts and emotions, creating a safe space for communication.

Practice Empathy

Try to put yourself in your partner's shoes. Imagine how they would feel in their situation and show understanding towards their concerns. Empathy builds emotional bridges and strengthens the bond between the two of you. Ask them how they feel and validate their emotions. A simple "I understand this is difficult for you" can make them feel understood and supported.

Use Clear and Reassuring Language

When you speak, use clear and calm language. Avoid using words or phrases that may increase their anxiety. Be honest and direct, but choose your words carefully so as not to provoke further concern. Use a calming tone to convey security and support. Emotional security is essential for effective communication.

Be Patient and Tolerant

Anxiety can cause your partner to need more time to process information and express their thoughts. Be patient and tolerant. Don't pressure them to talk if they don't feel ready, but make it clear that you're there when they're ready. Patience creates an environment where your partner feels safe to open up.

Avoid Criticism and Judgment

Criticism and judgment can exacerbate your partner's anxiety. Instead of pointing out what they might be doing wrong, focus on what they are doing right. Appreciate their efforts and value their bravery in facing anxiety. Positivity fosters trust and mutual understanding.

Offers Practical Support

In addition to words of encouragement, offer practical support. Ask them how you can help and respect their needs. Sometimes the simple act of being present and offering a helping hand can make all the difference. Offer to help with everyday tasks or find resources that might be helpful to them. Practical support shows that you are committed to making their trip more bearable.

Encourage Open Communication

Create an environment where open communication is welcome. Encourage your partner to share their thoughts and emotions with you. Reassure them that they are safe expressing themselves and that their feelings are valid. Trust in communication allows both to feel heard and understood.

Remember, anxiety does not define your partner, and with love, understanding, and effective communication, you can overcome challenges together. By practicing empathy and patience, you will be building a solid bridge to a stronger, more loving relationship.

Chapter 4: Intimacy in relationships with anxiety

Intimacy in relationships is like a delicate garden that needs care, patience and love to flourish. When anxiety hangs over this intimacy, it can seem like shadows obscure the connection between two people. However, it is crucial to understand that anxiety should not be an insurmountable obstacle, but rather an opportunity to strengthen emotional bonds and create even deeper and more meaningful intimacy.

The importance of intimacy in relationships

In the vast panorama of human relationships, intimacy stands as one of the fundamental pillars that support emotional connections between couples. It is not simply physical proximity, but a complex web of emotions, trust, openness and vulnerability that unites two individuals in deep and meaningful ways. Intimacy is not only a vital component of romantic relationships, but it is also essential for the growth and stability of the couple. Through this intricate journey into the human heart, we will explore the importance of intimacy in relationships and how its flourishing presence can transform a connection into something truly lasting and enriching.

Intimacy as the Foundation of the Relationship

At the core of every loving relationship, intimacy establishes a solid foundation upon which love flourishes. It is the process of revealing the deepest layers of our being, sharing our dreams, fears and hopes with our partner. This total openness creates a safe space where both individuals feel free to be authentic, without judgment or inhibitions. Intimacy is a brave act of vulnerability, a mutual gift of trust that strengthens the relationship and creates a bond that stands the tests of time.

Emotional Intimacy and its Transformative Power

Emotional intimacy goes beyond words and physical gestures; It is the ability to deeply understand another's emotions and respond with empathy. When couples share their most intimate thoughts and feelings, an emotional bond is established that creates a sense of belonging and security. Emotional intimacy transforms a relationship of companionship into a shared journey of personal and emotional growth. The trust and mutual understanding that come from emotional intimacy form a protective shield against storms that may threaten the relationship.

Physical Intimacy as a Manifestation of Love

Physical intimacy, although only part of the full spectrum of intimacy, is a profound expression of love and connection between couples. Through physical contact, bodies communicate in ways that words often cannot capture. Physical closeness not only encourages the release of love hormones, such as oxytocin , but also strengthens the emotional bond between lovers. Physical intimacy, properly understood and respected, is an act of love and mutual acceptance, which nourishes the relationship and reinforces the sense of togetherness.

Intimacy as a Healer of Emotional Wounds

In the human journey, we all carry emotional scars and wounds from the past. Intimacy in a relationship acts as a healing balm for these wounds. Unconditional acceptance and love shared in the intimate space allow couples to heal together, learn and grow from a place of vulnerability. Intimacy offers the opportunity to rediscover trust in oneself and in others, transforming wounds into strengths and scars into symbols of resilience .

Intimacy as a Spiritual Bond

In the depths of intimacy, there is a spiritual bond that transcends the physical and emotional. Spiritual connection is a recognition of soul mates, two beings who meet on a level of understanding and love that goes beyond earthly limitations. Spiritual intimacy nourishes the soul and strengthens the connection between couples, creating an experience of love that feels almost divine.

Intimacy as a Priceless Treasure

Ultimately, intimacy in relationships is a priceless treasure that deserves to be appreciated and protected. It is a journey of shared self-discovery, a process that nourishes, heals and transforms. As couples venture into the sacred ground of intimacy, they encounter a world of emotional and spiritual possibilities. In this intimate space, love blossoms, hearts intertwine and souls dance to the rhythm of an eternal connection. Intimacy is the most beautiful gift two people can offer each other, and in its presence, relationships rise to unimaginable heights, creating a bond that lasts forever in the fabric of time.

How to promote intimacy in a couple with anxiety

Anxiety can create a veil of worry and fear that sometimes seems difficult to break through. However, in the context of a relationship, anxiety should not be seen as an insurmountable obstacle, but rather as fertile ground where even deeper and more meaningful intimacy can flourish. Fostering intimacy in a couple facing anxiety requires not only love and patience, but also a deep understanding of each other's emotional and mental needs. It is a journey of mutual care and understanding, a process that can strengthen the bond and allow both individuals to feel safe and loved in the midst of their emotional challenges.

1. The Importance of Empathy

Empathy is the cornerstone on which intimacy is built in a couple affected by anxiety. Putting yourself in someone else's shoes, understanding their fears and concerns, essentially feeling the world through their eyes, creates an emotional bridge that connects people on a deep level. Empathy not only involves understanding the words that are said, but also reading unexpressed emotions, charged silences, and subtle gestures. When both partners practice empathy, it creates a space where they can freely share their thoughts and feelings, knowing that they will be understood and accepted without judgment.

2. Open and Honest Communication as a Foundation

Facing anxiety together starts with open and honest communication. Establishing an environment where you both feel safe to express your emotions is essential. It's important to talk about how each person feels and what specific challenges anxiety presents in the relationship. This frank communication not only increases mutual understanding, but also establishes a solid foundation for trust and emotional connection.

3. Vulnerability as Strength

In a relationship affected by anxiety, showing vulnerability is a show of courage. By sharing fears and insecurities, you create a space where you both feel free to be authentic. Being vulnerable involves not only sharing struggles, but also allowing the other to see the deepest parts of the soul. This mutual openness strengthens the bond, as both realize that they are loved and accepted even in their vulnerability.

4. Unconditional Support as an Emotional Anchor

Unconditional support is an invaluable gift in a relationship with anxiety. Knowing that the other is there in good times and bad, that they are willing to provide unreserved support, creates a feeling of emotional security. This means not judging or trying to change the other, but being present, listening, and offering comfort when necessary. This unconditional support builds a sense of security that allows both partners to face the challenges of anxiety together, knowing that they are not alone on their journey.

5. Patience as a Virtue

Anxiety can make people more sensitive, withdrawn, or reactive. In this context, patience becomes an essential virtue. It is important to give space when necessary and allow the other person to process their emotions at their own pace. Patience involves understanding that recovery times can vary and that everyone has their own journey to healing. This patience not only helps maintain peace in the relationship, but also fosters a sense of security, allowing both partners to feel free to be themselves without fear of judgment or impatience.

6. Creativity in Mutual Care

Fostering intimacy in a couple with anxiety can also be a creative process. Finding unique ways to connect can strengthen your bond. They can be small gestures, like writing notes of encouragement, preparing a special meal, or creating a quiet space to relax together. These actions show care and attention, and can be a balm for worried souls.

A Bond Strengthened by Adversity

Ultimately, fostering intimacy in a couple with anxiety is a journey of love, care, and understanding. Through empathy, open communication, vulnerability, unconditional support, patience and creativity, the emotional bond can be strengthened even in the midst of challenges. Instead of being an obstacle, anxiety can be seen as an opportunity to cultivate even deeper and more meaningful intimacy. When both partners support each other in their moments of vulnerability, they create a bond that is unbreakable, even in the face of emotional storms. On this shared journey, intimacy becomes a beacon of light, illuminating the path to a deeper, more loving connection.

Fostering intimacy in a couple with anxiety is not only possible, but it can strengthen your relationship in unimaginable ways. Through mutual care, unconditional acceptance, and patience, intimacy becomes a testament to the strength of love and the resilience of the human spirit. In the midst of anxiety, they can find a connection that goes beyond words, an intimacy that transcends everyday worries and is rooted in the true essence of being human. Ultimately, this intimacy is a precious gift, a rare gem found only in relationships where love is stronger than fear, and where mutual understanding becomes a bond that never breaks.

As you embrace this journey of intimacy in the midst of anxiety, you will find unwavering strength in shared love. Every challenge overcome, every moment of vulnerability faced, and every show of mutual support will weave an additional thread into the fabric of your relationship. Anxiety can be an unwanted guest in your relationship, but it can also be a powerful teacher, teaching you the importance of true connection and love that overcomes all barriers. At every step of this journey, remember that you are in this together, strengthening each other as you walk toward an intimacy that can only be found in the courageous embrace of shared vulnerability.

So, as you continue your journey together , allow intimacy to be your guide and your refuge. In every loving look, in every warm hug and in every word whispered in each other's ears, you will find the promise of a love that is true, deep and eternal. Intimacy in the midst of anxiety is a testament to your love and your courage to face life's challenges together. In every moment of connection, you will find peace and the certainty that you are exactly where you are meant to be: in each other's arms, building a love that overcomes all obstacles and flourishes even in the darkest corners of the soul.

This concludes the journey towards intimacy in a relationship affected by anxiety. May this path lead you to a deeper connection, to a love that is eternal and to an intimacy that is truly unbreakable. May your relationship be a beacon of hope and love, an inspiration to others who also face similar challenges. At every step, remember that the love you share is an unstoppable force, capable of brightening even the darkest days and guiding you toward a future filled with love, understanding, and an intimacy that lasts forever.

Chapter 5: How to build healthy relationships in uncertain times

In the dance of life, relationships face unexpected challenges and times of uncertainty. Whether it's personal challenges, economic crises, or global events that shake the foundations of our lives, relationships can be severely tested. However, in the midst of uncertainty, there is an opportunity to build healthy relationships that not only survive the storms, but also flourish and grow stronger.

Let's remember before continuing:

1. Resilience as a Fundamental Pillar

In uncertain times, resilience becomes a fundamental pillar in healthy relationships. Resilience involves the ability to adapt, recover and grow even in the face of adversity. Resilient couples do not give up in the face of difficulties; instead, they find creative ways to overcome challenges. They learn together, support each other, and hold on to hope even in the darkest of times. Resilience strengthens the bond, allowing the relationship to grow stronger as you overcome together the trials that life throws your way .

2. Clear and Open Communication

Clear and open communication is the foundation on which healthy relationships are built in uncertain times. Couples should be willing to talk about their fears, hopes, and challenges. Actively listening to your partner, without prejudice, and expressing your own feelings honestly creates an environment of trust and understanding. In times of uncertainty, effective communication becomes a beacon that guides the couple through the storm.

3. Empathy and Mutual Understanding

Empathy and mutual understanding are essential to building healthy relationships in uncertain times. Putting yourself in someone else's shoes, understanding their concerns and fears, and offering emotional support creates an indestructible bond. Empathy allows both partners to feel seen and understood in the midst of their individual and collective struggles. By understanding each other's emotions, a deep connection is established that acts as an emotional anchor, providing comfort and strength in times of uncertainty.

4. Adaptability as a Crucial Skill

In a rapidly changing world, adaptability becomes a crucial skill in healthy relationships. Couples must be willing to adjust to new circumstances and find creative ways to keep the spark in their relationship alive. This may involve discovering new ways to spend time together , exploring shared hobbies, or reinventing the way you connect emotionally. The ability to adapt together strengthens the bond and demonstrates the strength of the relationship.

5. Trust as an Essential Pillar

Trust is an essential pillar in all healthy relationships, especially in uncertain times. Mutual trust creates a sense of security and stability in the relationship. Couples must trust that each other is there to support, understand, and face challenges together. Trust involves belief in the strength of the relationship and the ability to overcome any adversity that comes along the way.

6. Gratitude and Appreciation for the Little Things

In the midst of uncertainty, practicing gratitude and appreciating the little things becomes a balm for the soul. Recognizing and valuing loving gestures, kind words, and moments of connection creates a positive environment in the relationship. Gratitude strengthens the emotional bond and fosters a sense of mutual appreciation. By focusing on the positive things, couples can find strength and joy even in the most challenging times.

7. Personal and Shared Growth

In uncertain times, personal and shared growth becomes a vital aspect of healthy relationships. Couples should encourage and support each other's individual growth, as well as grow together as a couple. This may involve learning new skills together , setting shared goals, or embarking on adventures that strengthen your bond. Personal and shared growth creates an enriching dynamic in the relationship and allows you to face the future with confidence and determination.

Strength in the Union

Ultimately, building healthy relationships in uncertain times is about finding strength in togetherness. Couples who face challenges together, support each other, and cultivate a deep connection discover a resilience that allows them to overcome any adversity. The relationship becomes a safe haven in the midst of the storm, a place where both partners find comfort, love and support.

On this journey toward building healthy relationships in uncertain times, each challenge overcome strengthens the bond. Every moment of shared vulnerability creates a deeper intimacy. Every expression of love and support for each other lights the way to a future full of hope and possibility. As they face challenges together, the couples discover that their union is truly unbreakable. Every step of the way, they realize that they are writing their own love story, a story of strength, courage, and a love that prevails even in the most uncertain of times.

Thus, in the midst of uncertainty, couples can build relationships that are resilient , loving, and deeply meaningful. With each challenge, they find an opportunity to grow together and strengthen their bond. Ultimately, building healthy relationships in uncertain times is about embracing adversity as an opportunity to strengthen the love you share. At every moment, they find strength in their union, proving that together they can overcome any challenge that comes their way. As they face uncertainty, they realize that their relationship is a beacon of hope and love in an often unpredictable world.

On this journey toward building healthy relationships in uncertain times, every experience, whether joyful or challenging, becomes an opportunity to learn and grow. Couples who embrace adversity with courage and love discover that they can overcome any obstacle. They find strength in their shared vulnerability and confidence in their ability to face the future together .

The Path Towards a Solid Future:

As they dive into building healthy relationships in uncertain times, couples discover the transformative power of love, open communication, and mutual support. They realize that even in the midst of challenges, their relationship can flourish and prosper. They find comfort in the fact that they are not alone, that they have someone by their side to share the joys and sorrows of life.

This path to a strong future is paved with mutual respect, trust, and gratitude for shared love. Couples who strive to build healthy relationships in uncertain times find deep peace in their union. Every day becomes an opportunity to strengthen your emotional connection and build meaningful memories together.

The Strength in the Union:

Ultimately, the strength of a relationship lies in the union of two souls who choose to walk together even on the most difficult paths. Couples who face uncertainty with courage and compassion find indestructible strength in their love for each other. They support each other in difficult times and celebrate together in happy moments.

The relationship becomes a safe haven, a place where they can be themselves without fear of judgment. They find comfort in each other's arms and discover that their love is an inexhaustible source of positive energy. With each challenge overcome, they realize that their bond has grown stronger and that their love is deeper than ever.

Build relationships

Building healthy relationships in uncertain times is a journey that requires dedication, patience, and unconditional love. Couples who are willing to face challenges together, who communicate openly and honestly, and who support each other every step of the way, discover a connection that is truly eternal.

As you continue your journey together , remember that your love is the foundation on which you can build a strong and meaningful future. Each challenge overcome brings them closer to each other and strengthens their emotional bond. With each shared experience, you grow as individuals and as a couple. Ultimately, healthy relationships in uncertain times are a testament to the power of love and human resilience .

Thus concludes this journey towards building healthy relationships in the midst of uncertainty. May every couple who embraces this journey find the strength and love necessary to overcome any challenge that comes their way. In every step, may you find joy in your connection to each other and comfort in the fact that you are facing the future together. In every moment, may you find peace in your shared love and the certainty that your relationship is a beacon of hope in an often bewildering world. With love, communication, and mutual support, each couple can build a strong, lasting future, even in the midst of uncertainty.

Thus concludes this journey towards building healthy relationships in the midst of uncertainty. May every couple who embraces this journey find the strength and love necessary to overcome any challenge that comes their way. In every step, may you find joy in your connection to each other and comfort in the fact that you are facing the future together. In every moment, may you find peace in your shared love and the certainty that your relationship is a beacon of hope in an often bewildering world. With love, communication, and mutual support, each couple can build a strong, lasting future, even in the midst of uncertainty.

How to deal with uncertainty in relationships

Uncertainty is an inevitable part of life, and relationships are not exempt from this challenge. Uncertainty can arise from a variety of sources: unexpected life changes, important decisions to be made, economic challenges, or even global events that affect society as a whole. In the context of a relationship, uncertainty can generate anxiety, tension and doubts about the future. However, dealing with uncertainty effectively is essential to maintaining a strong and healthy relationship. Here I present practical strategies to overcome the challenges that uncertainty can present in a relationship:

1. Open Communication and Honesty:

One of the fundamental keys to facing uncertainty in a relationship is to maintain open and honest communication. Both partners should feel safe to express their concerns, fears, and expectations regarding the uncertainty they face. Talking clearly about feelings and insecurities can help dispel misunderstandings and strengthen the emotional bond.

2. Set Goals and Plan Together:

In the face of uncertainty, it is crucial to establish clear goals and objectives as a couple. This may involve setting financial goals, planning for your family's future, or deciding how to face the challenges ahead together. Working together to establish a plan of action can provide a sense of purpose and control in the midst of uncertainty.

3. Build Individual and Collective Resilience :

Resilience is the ability to adapt and recover from challenges. Promoting resilience both individually and as a couple can help you face uncertainty with greater emotional strength. This involves developing skills to manage stress, learning to see challenges as opportunities for growth, and cultivating a positive mindset even in difficult times.

4. Practice Empathy and Understanding:

Uncertainty can generate intense and sometimes contradictory emotions. It is essential to practice empathy and mutual understanding. Trying to put yourself in the other person's shoes, understand their concerns, and show emotional support can strengthen emotional connection and reduce the feeling of isolation that uncertainty can cause.

5. Manage Anxiety and Stress:

Uncertainty can trigger anxiety and stress in both partners. It is important to develop effective strategies to manage these emotions, whether through regular practice of relaxation techniques such as meditation or yoga, physical exercise, or even seeking professional support such as couples or individual therapy.

6. Build a Support Network:

Facing uncertainty doesn't mean doing it alone as a couple. Building a support network that includes friends, family, or even other couples can provide an invaluable support system. Talking to people who have faced similar challenges can provide unique perspectives and emotional comfort.

7. Practice Gratitude and Appreciation:

In the midst of uncertainty, it is easy to focus on what is missing or the challenges ahead. Practicing gratitude and appreciation for the little things can change your perspective. Recognizing and celebrating small victories, kind gestures, and everyday joys can increase relationship positivity and strengthen emotional resilience .

8. Accept that Uncertainty is a Natural Part of Life:

Finally, it is crucial to accept that uncertainty is a natural part of life. Despite our best efforts and planning, we cannot predict or control everything that happens in the future. Accepting this truth can help release the need for absolute control and allow the couple to adapt and grow together in the face of the unknown.

Facing uncertainty in a relationship is a continuous process that requires patience, communication and emotional openness. By implementing these practical strategies and cultivating an attitude of collaboration and mutual support, couples can not only survive the challenges of uncertainty, but also strengthen their relationship and grow together in the process.

Uncertainty as an opportunity

Uncertainty, far from being simply an obstacle that we must overcome, can be seen as an opportunity for personal growth and as a couple. Facing the unknown together can strengthen emotional bonds and create a solid foundation for the future. Here are some ways in which uncertainty can be seen as an opportunity in a relationship:

1. Promotes Adaptability:

In a world that is constantly changing, the ability to adapt has become an invaluable resource. Uncertainty in relationships offers the opportunity to develop adaptability skills. Learning to adjust expectations and plans based on changing circumstances can strengthen your relationship and improve your ability to face future challenges together.

2. Promotes Open Communication:

Uncertainty requires open and honest communication. Couples are forced to talk about their fears, hopes and expectations for the future. This openness in communication not only strengthens the current relationship, but also lays the foundation for effective communication in future challenges. Learning to express concerns and listen to your partner in an understanding way can lead to greater emotional intimacy.

3. Strengthens Mutual Trust:

In the midst of uncertainty, mutual trust becomes an invaluable asset. Trusting that your partner is there to support, listen and understand creates an environment of emotional security. Mutual trust not only helps to cope with current uncertainty, but also establishes a solid foundation to face future challenges with courage and confidence.

4. Cultivate Emotional Resilience :

resilience , the ability to recover from adversity, is strengthened when facing uncertainty as a couple. Couples who can overcome challenges together develop greater emotional resilience. This sense of resilience not only benefits the current relationship, but also equips each individual to handle future uncertainties with greater confidence and determination.

5. Promotes Empathy and Understanding:

Uncertainty can generate a range of complex emotions, from fear to anxiety and frustration. By facing these feelings together, couples can cultivate empathy and understanding. Understanding each other's emotions and being able to show empathy creates a deeper and more meaningful bond. This emotional connection can be an invaluable asset in the relationship and can help you overcome future challenges.

6. Motivates Creativity and Innovation:

When circumstances change and uncertainty prevails, couples are motivated to be creative and innovative in the way they approach problems. Thinking outside the box, considering new perspectives, and being willing to try new solutions are valuable skills that are developed in the midst of uncertainty. These skills can be applied not only in the relationship, but also in other aspects of life.

7. Foster a Sense of Shared Adventure:

Instead of being seen as a burden, uncertainty can be embraced as a shared adventure. Navigating the unknown together can be exciting and can strengthen a couple's sense of camaraderie. Seeing uncertainty as a natural part of life and being willing to face it together can infuse the relationship with a renewed sense of purpose and unity.

8. Promotes Individual and Mutual Growth:

Ultimately, uncertainty can be seen as a catalyst for individual and mutual growth. By facing challenges and overcoming adversity together, couples can discover new strengths within themselves and their relationship. This continued growth can lead to greater satisfaction in the relationship and can help build a solid foundation for the future.

Uncertainty in relationships can be seen as an opportunity to strengthen emotional connection, promote resilience , and cultivate a shared sense of adventure. Through open communication, mutual trust, empathy, and creativity, couples can not only weather current challenges, but also grow and thrive together. Instead of being feared, uncertainty can be embraced as a driving force for the growth and enrichment of the relationship. With courage and determination, couples can transform uncertain times into opportunities to strengthen their love and build a relationship that is resilient and meaningful.

How to overcome relationship challenges in uncertain times

Uncertainty, that state of ignorance about what is to come, can deeply affect our relationships. Uncertain situations, whether caused by global events, changes in our personal lives, or economic challenges, can cause stress and strain in the relationship. However, facing uncertainty as a couple is possible and can strengthen your bond. Here are some practical strategies to overcome the challenges of relationships in uncertain times:

1. Understand the Nature of Uncertainty:

Uncertainty is a constant reality in our lives. Accepting that the future is inherently uncertain can help reduce anxiety. Recognizing that we all face uncertain times at different stages of our lives can create a sense of universality and connection with others.

2. Encourage Open Communication:

Open and honest communication is the cornerstone of any strong relationship. In uncertain times, it is crucial to talk openly about fears, worries and expectations. Take the time to listen to your partner without judgment and express your own emotions clearly and respectfully. Effective communication can dispel misunderstandings and strengthen emotional connection.

3. Establish Routines and Structure:

In uncertain times, routines can provide a sense of normality and stability. Try to maintain certain daily routines, such as meal times or time for shared activities. Establishing structure in your day-to-day life can create a sense of control and predictability in the midst of uncertainty.

4. Practice Empathy and Understanding:

Uncertainty can generate a variety of emotions, from fear to frustration. Practicing empathy means putting yourself in someone else's shoes and trying to understand their emotions and perspectives. Mutual understanding can strengthen the emotional connection and help both partners feel supported and understood.

5. Find Creative Ways to Connect:

Although circumstances may limit social and leisure activities, finding creative ways to connect is essential. You could explore new hobbies together at home, cook together, watch movies or shows you both enjoy, or even plan future adventures for when the situation stabilizes. These shared activities can strengthen your relationship and provide moments of joy.

6. Set Realistic Goals:

Facing uncertainty can be less overwhelming when you set realistic goals. This could involve short-term financial goals, plans to improve skills, or even goals related to the relationship itself. Setting achievable goals can provide a sense of direction and achievement.

7. Learn to Manage Stress:

Stress is a common reaction to uncertainty. Learning stress management techniques, such as deep breathing, meditation, or regular exercise, can help you stay calm and face challenges with mental clarity. Consider practicing these techniques together to support each other.

8. Seek Professional Support if Necessary:

Sometimes facing uncertainty can be overwhelming and can put a strain on your relationship. If you feel that the situation is too difficult to handle on your own, do not hesitate to seek professional support. A therapist or counselor can provide specific tools and strategies to deal with stress and uncertainty as a couple.

9. Cultivate Gratitude and Appreciation:

In the midst of uncertainty, it can be easy to focus on what is missing or what is out of your control. Practicing gratitude involves recognizing and appreciating the small positive things in life and in your relationship. You can do this by verbally expressing what you appreciate about each other or by keeping a gratitude journal to record happy moments and daily accomplishments.

10. Remember that you are a Team:

Ultimately, remember that you and your partner are a team. Facing uncertainty together can strengthen your bond and demonstrate your ability to overcome challenges as a couple. Maintain a collaborative approach, support each other, and remember that as a team you can overcome any obstacle.

Facing uncertainty in a relationship requires a combination of open communication, mutual support, and emotional resilience . By applying these practical strategies and maintaining a positive attitude, you can overcome the challenges of uncertain times and strengthen your relationship. Remember that every couple is unique, so adapt these strategies based on the specific needs and dynamics of your relationship. With patience, love, and determination, you can overcome any challenge and build a strong, long-lasting relationship.

Closing

As we come to the end of our journey together through the complexities of love in times of anxiety and uncertainty, it's natural to feel a mix of emotions. On this journey, we explore the depths of the human heart and discover how anxiety can color our closest relationships with shades of worry and fear. However, we also discover the resilience of love and how, even in the most challenging times, true connections can flourish and grow stronger.

In the opening chapter, we understood that anxiety can manifest itself in various ways, from mild restlessness to paralyzing panic, and how these nuances can affect our couple dynamics. We explore symptoms, from palpable tension to emotional turmoil, understanding how these signs can influence our everyday interactions.

We delve into the roots of anxiety in the context of relationships. From the scars of the past to the pressures of the present, from unmet expectations to worries about the future, each cause revealed a fundamental truth: our emotions are intricate and our relationships are vulnerable. However, these vulnerabilities do not weaken our connections; in fact, they are the very essence of our shared humanity.

At the heart of our exploration lies communication, the thread that weaves the tapestry of our relationships. We learned how anxiety can distort our words, creating misunderstandings and leaving room for doubt. But we also learned that, with empathy and patience, communication can become a beacon of light in the midst of emotional darkness. Listening with understanding and speaking with tenderness can heal emotional wounds and strengthen the ties between souls.

Intimacy, that delicate dance of naked souls, was another crucial theme. We discover how anxiety can create barriers in our most intimate moments, transforming closeness into a terrain of uncertainty. However, we also learned how mutual acceptance and understanding can transform these obstacles into opportunities for deeper, more meaningful love.

In the last leg of our journey, we face uncertainty, that universal challenge that comes in different forms. We recognized that while uncertainty can create fear, it can also be an opportunity for growth. By accepting the unknown and embracing the fluid nature of life, we can find strength in adaptability and love in each other's company.

Now, as I close this book, I invite you to take with you not only the lessons learned, but also the compassionate spirit with which they were taught. May these words accompany you in your days, reminding you that love, in its purest form, is a beacon of hope in dark times. May open communication and mutual understanding be your constant allies, and may you find the strength to embrace uncertainty as an opportunity to grow and love more deeply.

Ultimately, remember that love in times of anxiety and uncertainty is not perfect; It is peppered with challenges and adorned with imperfections. But it is these same imperfections that make our love authentic and meaningful. So move forward, with courage and compassion, knowing that in every beat of your heart and every shared breath, lies the unbreakable force of true love.

With love and hope, Olivia

Don't miss out!

Visit the website below and you can sign up to receive emails whenever Olivia I. Thigpen (ENG) publishes a new book. There's no charge and no obligation.

https://books2read.com/r/B-A-MBHBB-DIVRC

BOOKS2READ

Connecting independent readers to independent writers.

Did you love *Love amidst Anxiety: How to Build Healthy Relationships in Uncertain Times*? Then you should read *Breaking Free from Narcissistic Manipulation: Strategies for Healing and Thriving Beyond Toxic Relationships*[1] by Olivia Thigpen!

This transformative book will guide you through a journey of deep healing, helping you break free from the clutches of narcissistic relationships and flourish into a life filled with self-love and healthy relationships.

Immerse yourself in the pages of this book and learn to recognize the signs of toxic relationships, overcome low self-esteem, establish healthy boundaries, and cultivate empowering emotional resilience. With practical strategies backed by experience and expert knowledge, you will discover how to heal emotional wounds and build a life full of love, confidence, and positivity.

This book is much more than a self-discovery guide; is a beacon of hope for those who have suffered in manipulative relationships. Discover how

---

1. https://books2read.com/u/bzBQ62

2. https://books2read.com/u/bzBQ62

self-acceptance, self-care, and resilience can transform your life and lead you to genuine and fulfilling relationships.

Don't miss the opportunity to free yourself from the past, heal your wounds, and embrace a future full of self-love and meaningful connections.

<u>Change your life today with "Break Free from Narcissistic Manipulation" and begin the journey to a new and better version of yourself!</u>

Also by Olivia I. Thigpen (ENG)

Healthy Mind
The Overthinking Cure: 8 Proven Strategies to Free Your Mind from Negative Spirals, Reduce Stress, Boost Productivity, and Live in the Present Moment
Love amidst Anxiety: How to Build Healthy Relationships in Uncertain Times

Healthy Relationships
Breaking Free from Narcissistic Manipulation: Strategies for Healing and Thriving Beyond Toxic Relationships
Narcissistic Relationships: Overcoming Codependency, Setting Boundaries, and Healing Romantic Bonds in a Turbulent World

About the Author

Olivia I. Thigpen is a frenetic, multitasking woman. She began her career as an elementary school teacher, but her passion for psychology led her down a different path. She decided to pursue a bachelor's degree in psychology and it wasn't long before she became a psychiatrist. Her experience in her field gave her a wealth of knowledge that would later prove invaluable to her in her career as a writer.